W9-BBQ-632

A Day with an Electrician

By Mark Thomas

Welcome Books

Children's Press
A Division of Grolier Publishing
New York / London / Hong Kong / Sydney
Danbury, Connecticut

Photo Credits: Cover and all photos by Maura Boruchow
Contributing Editor: Jeri Cipriano
Book Design: Christopher Logan

Visit Children's Press on the Internet at:
http://publishing.grolier.com

Cataloging-in-Publication Data

Library of Congress Cataloging-in-Publication Data

Thomas, Mark, 1963-
  A day with an electrician / by Mark Thomas.
    p. cm.—(Hard work)
  Includes bibliographical references and index.
  ISBN 0-516-23140-5 (lib. bdg.)—ISBN 0-516-23065-4 (pbk.)
  1. Electricians—Vocational guidance—Juvenile literature. [1. Electricians. 2.
Occupations.] I. Title. II. Series.

TK159 .T46 2000
621.319'24'023—dc21

00-057033

Copyright © 2001 by Rosen Book Works, Inc.
All rights reserved. Published simultaneously in Canada.
Printed in the United States of America.
1 2 3 4 5 6 7 8 9 10 R 05 04 03 02 01

Contents

My name is Peter.

I am an **electrician**.

I help give **electric power** to your home.

This room needs a light to make it bright.

A light has **wires** that make it work.

I tie the two red wires.

Then I tie the two black wires.

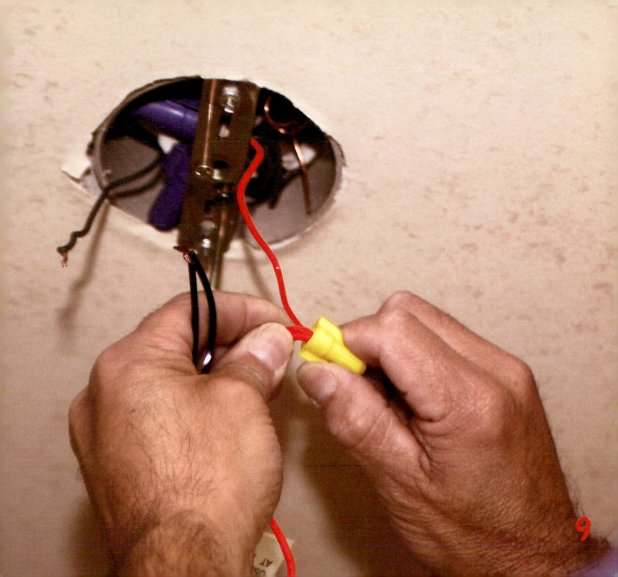

9

I put in a **light bulb**.

11

I put the cover
over the light bulb.

12

Now I put in a **light switch**.

The switch will make the light turn on and off.

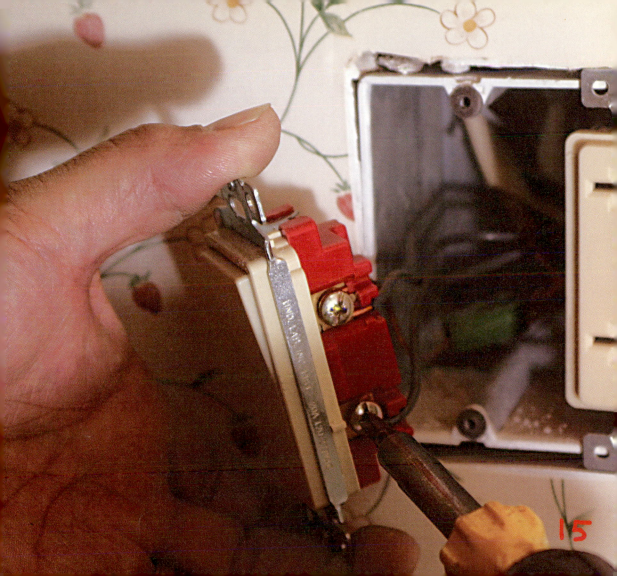

15

I need **screws** to hold the light switch to the wall.

I use a **screwdriver** to put in the screws.

17

I turn on the light.

It works!

The room is nice and bright.

I like bringing light to your home.

I like being an electrician.

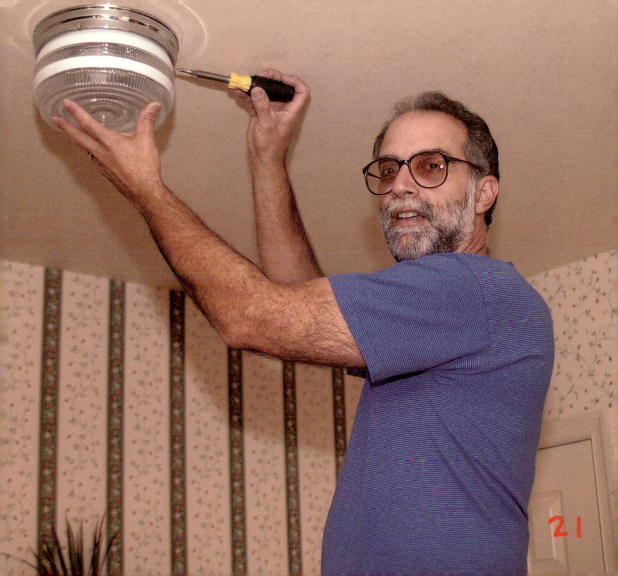

New Words

electrician (eh-lek-**trih**-shun) a person who works with wires and electric lights

electric power (eh-**lek**-trik **pow**-er) a form of energy that produces light

light bulb (**lyt buhlb**) something that gives off light

light switch (**lyt swich**) something that lets you turn a light on or off

screwdriver (**scroo**-dryv-er) a tool used to turn screws

screws (**scrooz**) metal pins used to hold things together

wires (**weye**-erz) thin pieces of metal that carry electric power to a light

22

To Find Out More

Books
Batteries, Bulbs, and Wires
by David Glover
Kingfisher Books

Discovering Electricity
by Rae Bains and Joel Snyder
Troll Communications

Web Site
What Do They Do: Electrician
http://www.whatdotheydo.com/electric.htm
You can read about what electricians do and where they work at this Web site.

23

Index

About the Author

Mark Thomas is a writer and educator who lives in Florida. He has built and repaired things in and around his home most of his life.

Reading Consultants

Kris Flynn, Coordinator, Small School District Literacy, The San Diego County Office of Education

Shelly Forys, Certified Reading Recovery Specialist, W.J. Zahnow Elementary School, Waterloo, IL

Peggy McNamara, Professor, Bank Street College of Education, Reading and Literacy Program

DISCARDED

J 621.319 THOMAS
Thomas, Mark
Day with an electrician

PEACHTREE

Atlanta-Fulton Public Library

NOV 2 0 2001